THE TWELVE CAROLS OF Christmas

The favorites, full piano and words sheet

Arranged by

Nolene Prince

Published in Australia by
RCM Publications
info@resource.com.au
www.resource.com.au

The Twelve Carols of Christmas, The favorites, full piano and words sheet.
arranged by Nolene Prince © Copyright 1986, 2002, 2020
First published under the title Carols we Love to Sing. Revised and updated.

National Library of Australia Cataloguing in Publication entry

 A catalogue record for this
book is available from the
National Library of Australia

ISBN 978-0-9804850-9-7

Cover design by Mahesh Dunukara
Interior layout by Sophie White Design
Printed by Kindle Direct Publishing

1 Brown   2 Red Brown   3 Lt. Brown

4 Red   5 Orange   6 Yellow

7 Dark Green   8 Green   9 Lt. Green

10 Blue   11 Turquoise   12 Lt. Blue

13 Purple   14 Lavender   15 Magenta

16 Hot Pink   17 Pink   18 Peach

19 Grey   20 Dark Grey   21 Black

1 Brown 2 Red Brown 3 Lt. Brown

4 Red 5 Orange 6 Yellow

7 Dark Green 8 Green 9 Lt. Green

10 Blue 11 Turquoise 12 Lt. Blue

13 Purple 14 Lavender 15 Magenta

16 Hot Pink 17 Pink 18 Peach

19 Grey 20 Dark Grey 21 Black

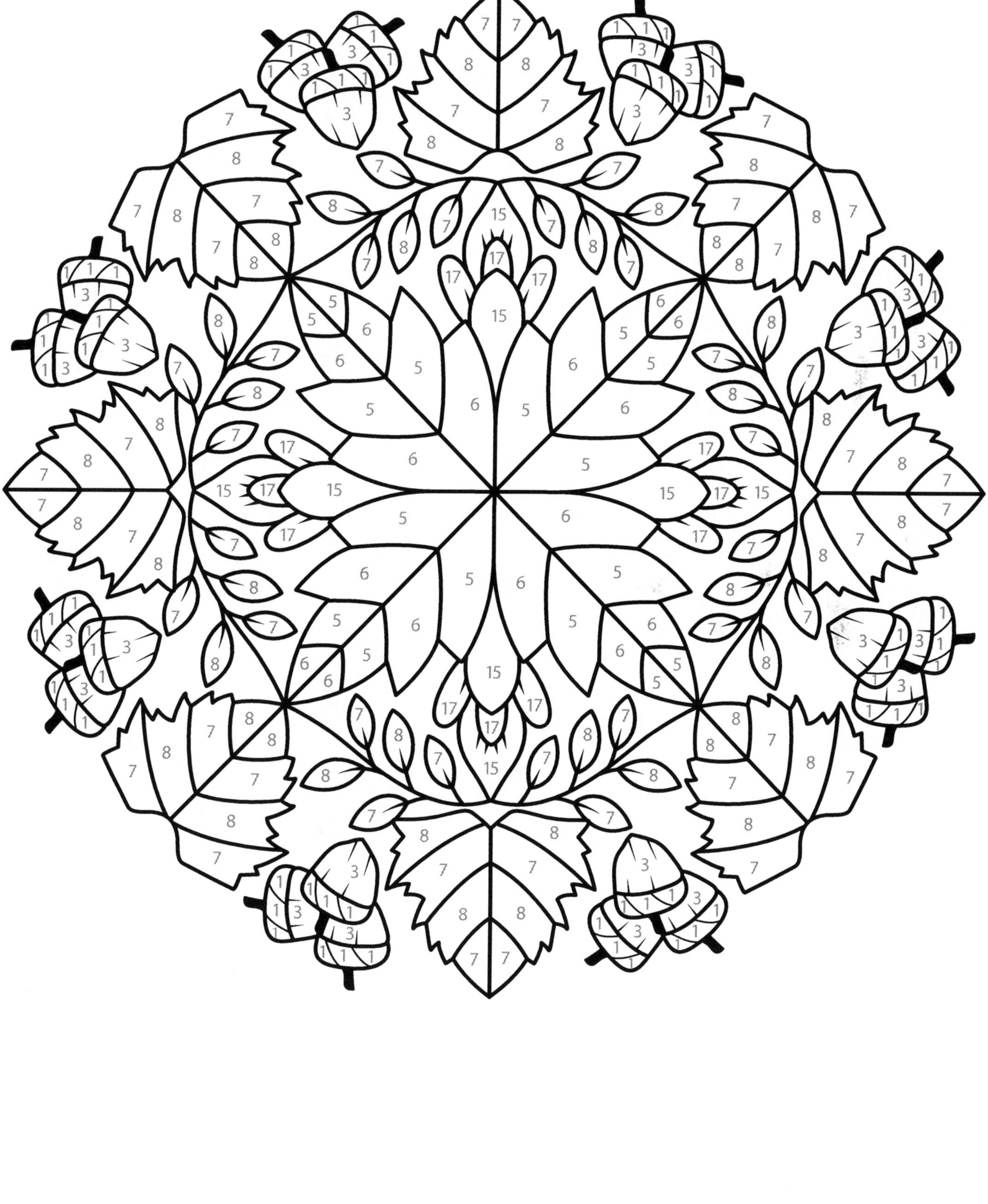

1 Brown	2 Red Brown	3 Lt. Brown
4 Red	5 Orange	6 Yellow
7 Dark Green	8 Green	9 Lt. Green
10 Blue	11 Turquoise	12 Lt. Blue
13 Purple	14 Lavender	15 Magenta
16 Hot Pink	17 Pink	18 Peach
19 Grey	20 Dark Grey	21 Black

1 Brown	2 Red Brown	3 Lt. Brown
4 Red	5 Orange	6 Yellow
7 Dark Green	8 Green	9 Lt. Green
10 Blue	11 Turquoise	12 Lt. Blue
13 Purple	14 Lavender	15 Magenta
16 Hot Pink	17 Pink	18 Peach
19 Grey	20 Dark Grey	21 Black

1 Brown	2 Red Brown	3 Lt. Brown
4 Red	5 Orange	6 Yellow
7 Dark Green	8 Green	9 Lt. Green
10 Blue	11 Turquoise	12 Lt. Blue
13 Purple	14 Lavender	15 Magenta
16 Hot Pink	17 Pink	18 Peach
19 Grey	20 Dark Grey	21 Black

1 Brown	2 Red Brown	3 Lt. Brown
4 Red	5 Orange	6 Yellow
7 Dark Green	8 Green	9 Lt. Green
10 Blue	11 Turquoise	12 Lt. Blue
13 Purple	14 Lavender	15 Magenta
16 Hot Pink	17 Pink	18 Peach
19 Grey	20 Dark Grey	21 Black

1	Brown	2	Red Brown	3	Lt. Brown
4	Red	5	Orange	6	Yellow
7	Dark Green	8	Green	9	Lt. Green
10	Blue	11	Turquoise	12	Lt. Blue
13	Purple	14	Lavender	15	Magenta
16	Hot Pink	17	Pink	18	Peach
19	Grey	20	Dark Grey	21	Black

1	Brown	2	Red Brown	3	Lt. Brown
4	Red	5	Orange	6	Yellow
7	Dark Green	8	Green	9	Lt. Green
10	Blue	11	Turquoise	12	Lt. Blue
13	Purple	14	Lavender	15	Magenta
16	Hot Pink	17	Pink	18	Peach
19	Grey	20	Dark Grey	21	Black

1 Brown	2 Red Brown	3 Lt. Brown
4 Red	5 Orange	6 Yellow
7 Dark Green	8 Green	9 Lt. Green
10 Blue	11 Turquoise	12 Lt. Blue
13 Purple	14 Lavender	15 Magenta
16 Hot Pink	17 Pink	18 Peach
19 Grey	20 Dark Grey	21 Black

1 Brown
2 Red Brown
3 Lt. Brown
4 Red
5 Orange
6 Yellow
7 Dark Green
8 Green
9 Lt. Green
10 Blue
11 Turquoise
12 Lt. Blue
13 Purple
14 Lavender
15 Magenta
16 Hot Pink
17 Pink
18 Peach
19 Grey
20 Dark Grey
21 Black

1. Brown
2. Red Brown
3. Lt. Brown
4. Red
5. Orange
6. Yellow
7. Dark Green
8. Green
9. Lt. Green
10. Blue
11. Turquoise
12. Lt. Blue
13. Purple
14. Lavender
15. Magenta
16. Hot Pink
17. Pink
18. Peach
19. Grey
20. Dark Grey
21. Black

1 Brown	2 Red Brown	3 Lt. Brown
4 Red	5 Orange	6 Yellow
7 Dark Green	8 Green	9 Lt. Green
10 Blue	11 Turquoise	12 Lt. Blue
13 Purple	14 Lavender	15 Magenta
16 Hot Pink	17 Pink	18 Peach
19 Grey	20 Dark Grey	21 Black

Made in the USA
Las Vegas, NV
04 November 2023

80239095R00017